The Drakoo

A Collection of Children's Poetry

Written and illustrated by **Elle Youn**
With contributions from **Juliet Youn**

Shooting

When I was shooting my bow and my arrow
I looked at the target so small and so narrow
I aimed at the bullseye
I fired the arrow
But wouldn't you know the thing hit a sparrow

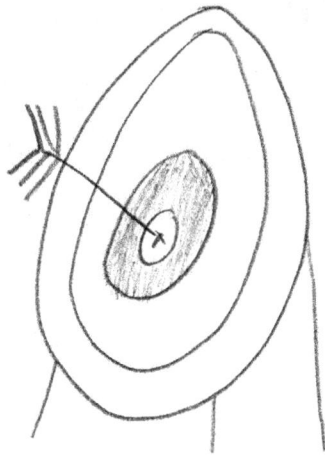

Paul

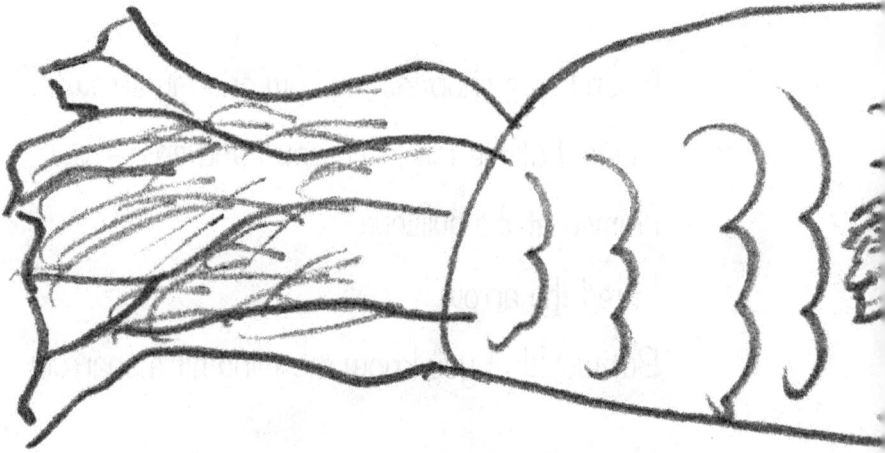

I have a best friend

    He is my pet

        He loves to swim

            He is all wet

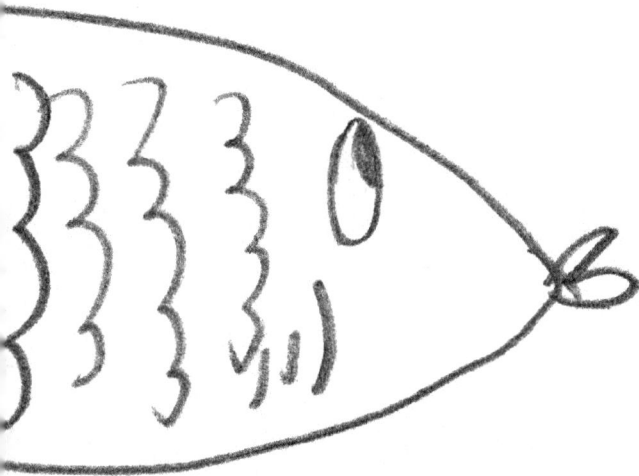

I try to feed him

  every day

    he loves to swim

      and sleep and play

Fireworks

I used to call them Fire Booms!

Their smoke made a mess in the sky

But now I know they're Fireworks

Boom boom boom my oh my

My Uniform

I wake up in the morning and I put on my shirt

I put on my shorts and I put on my skirt

My socks, my shoes, and my backpack too

Then I brush my hair and I'm ready for school!

Baseball

Baseball is a game that is played in the fall
You score lots of points hitting bat to ball
If you love winning you'll love this game
Any other sport just isn't the same

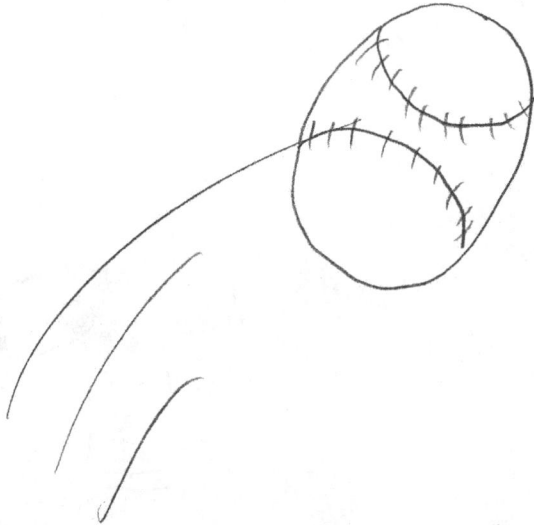

Beware the Bear!

Mr. Bear, Mr. Bear, you have lots of hair

You eat naughty children, who lie and don't care

You dip them in honey, and gobble them up

These children who steal and complain and don't share

You search for the children who never obey

Who don't put their toys and their mittens away

So all of you children, you'd better beware

Of the Big, and the Bad, and the Fierce Mr. Bear

I love the stars at night

And I really hope they don't go away

I like that they shine bright

I wish they happened in the day

- by Juliet

Art

My favorite activity at school is Art

Flowers and roses and pretty parts

Painting and making a real big mess

Brings me joy and happiness

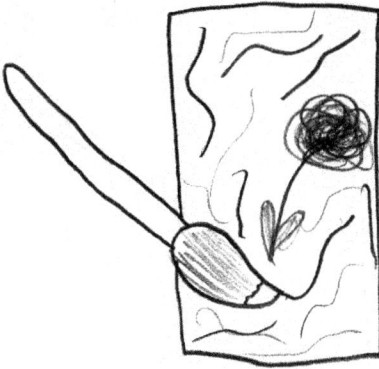

The Jeep

My daddy owns a jeep
It's blue and has 4 wheels
Just like a cow has legs
How very smooth it feels

There's carpet on the inside
The steering wheel is black
There are five seats for people
I sit in front, not back

My daddy takes me often
And we ride the jeep together
It's sometimes very windy
I feel like I'm a feather

I like that sometimes there's no top
And sometimes there's no doors
Except when it is going to rain
It drips onto the floors

When climbing over rocks and stuff
The jeep is very fun
I think everybody's dad
Should go out and buy one

Flying a Kite

Flying a kite is fun
I do it when it's windy
And even though I sometimes let go
I love kites when they go

The kites fly in the air
When I run through the fields
The ribbons are flying to and fro
I love kites when they go

Some have stripes and dots
Some have strings and bows
Mine is zigzagged, don't you know
I love kites when they go

My Daddy is the holder
Of the kite when I run
And even though I sometimes let go
I love kites when they go

Bald Eagle

There was a bald eagle whose name was Kyle

He was very, very, very wild

He loves to fly, and he flies right by

The house until I can't see him anymore

He fiercely guards the eggs in his nest

And when he's tired, he will rest

But when he dives for fish and mice

Then I'm able to see him soar

Butterfly - by Juliet

Ella is a butterfly
She loves to fly in the sky up high
She's blue and purple and likes to dance
On lilies, and roses, and tulip plants
She drinks the nectar from the flowers
And visits other bugs for hours
And when I see her flutter by
I feel like I'm a butterfly

Swimming - by Juliet

I like going swimming it's so much fun
I don't want to stop ever in my life

If I get out of the pool then I get very cold
So I don't want to stop ever in my life

I like the blue water and it's shiny too
And I don't want to stop ever in my life

But the chemicals make my eyes hurt
So I guess I should stop sometimes in my life

Every drop of water goes up

Vapor oh so clear

And liquid water just the same

Precipitation is rain

Over the earth

Rainbows appear

Above the houses

The water cycle

Is really cool

Oceans below, and clouds in the sky

Nature is all wet

The Drakoo

Drakoo is made up from my mind
Dragon wings and really kind
Unicorn horn on his heart shaped head
Webbed feet, spiked tail, and eyes of red

White and black with a bubble gum smell
Fat and furry and has a shell
Pointy teeth and funny looks
He sits all day and reads his books

I like to think of my Drakoo
When I have nothing else to do
And drawing him is lots of fun
If you're reading this, you should draw one

Book Respect

Books are beautiful and almost alive
They make you laugh out loud
They help you to learn and to survive
And can really draw a crowd

Hannah Banana

Once upon a time there was a girl named Hannah

Some people called her Hannah Banana

Hannah Banana thought it would be cool

To never have to go to school

So Hannah Banana, she learned nothing new

She never learned how to cut or glue

She couldn't write, she couldn't read

She couldn't sew, she couldn't knead

She never learned how to follow the rules

And always got kicked out of swimming pools

She never learned about maps and things
And dogs, and fish, and birds with wings
And Hannah Banana, she couldn't count
She never knew the right amount
And when she grew up, she couldn't cook
Because she couldn't read a book
And so the hungry girl did die
And everybody wondered why
Poor Hannah Banana was such a fool
For never wanting to go to school

A Poem For Daughters

Be the dreamers of dreams and the swingers of branches
Go play in the leaves where the pixie dust dances
Climb every mountain and ford every stream
Live all you can, make your life be a scream
Let the wind know you're here, that you matter, you lived.

Move the earth, let it move you
Keep your head in the clouds and your feet on the sand
See all you can see and do all that you can
Have faith in your friends and have hope for the future

Do all things with love.

For the branches that bend and the dreams that we dream
of the highest of peaks or the coolest of streams
of the birds on their wings and the kisses of fairies
mean nothing at all without love
- so love very.

~The Authors~

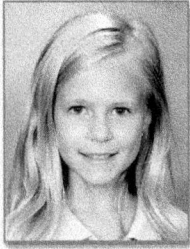

Elle is excited to present her second book. When she is not writing stories and drawing pictures, she loves to shoot her bow and arrow, dance with her younger sisters, and participate in Cub Scouts.

"I want people to know that I'm a big strong girl, because I _am_ a big strong girl, I am in kindergarten now! And guess what, I have been in kindergarten now for more than five days!" - Juliet

Written and illustrated by **Elle Youn**
Contributing works by **Juliet Youn**

Digitized, assembled, and published by Paper Airplane Books
www.PaperAirplaneBooks.com

"A Poem For Daughters" was written by the publisher and makes reference to many poems and works of other artists. We believe these references are "transformative" in nature and not substantial in scope to the comparative size of the poem as a whole. The references are meant to pay homage to the writers, thinkers, and poets that have come before us, who have helped make our world a better place.

Written, Published, and Printed in the USA!

Paper Airplane books - www.PaperAirplaneBooks.com